Living For Jesus

Book 1 – BEHAVED

Interactive & Inspirational Lessons
For Teens & Young Adults

Gloria Onoseremen Itua

Raising Adolescents with Godly Character

Author's Contact:
E-mail: gloriaitua@yahoo.com

Tellwell Talent
www.tellwell.ca

ISBN
978-0-2288-5144-8 (Hardcover)
978-0-2288-5145-5 (Paperback)
978-0-2288-5146-2 (eBook)

THIS BOOK IS A
SPECIAL GIFT

From

To

On the occasion of

Date

DEDICATION

To my beloved children.

CONTENTS

ACKNOWLEDGEMENTS

Thanks to my beloved children: Itohansose, Ofure and Ehinomen, whose presence, encouragement, and contribution in numerous ways brought the inspiration to write this book. Itohansose was part of the editing process. Ofure is the graphic designer. She designed the book cover artwork. Ehi was helpful with logistics.

Thanks to my mother, who has gone to be with the Lord. She always encouraged me to keep on writing. Keep resting in the bosom of our Lord Jesus Christ Mother.

Special thanks to my big brother, Dr. Ehinor Arhebamen, who also was a part of the editing process.

I also want to acknowledge and appreciate my husband for his support.

Most of all, thanks to God Almighty, who gave me the wisdom to write and present this work.

A MESSAGE TO PARENTS
AND EDUCATORS

The act of encouraging teens and young adults to read good books is a crucial factor in their psychological and intellectual development. It promotes a mutually warm and satisfying relationship between them and their parents and enhances their awareness of the world around them.

It stimulates teens' IMAGINATION and lays a FOUNDATION for the DEVELOPMENT of skills necessary to support the critical THINKING process.

In addition, the parent who encourages their teen and young adult children to read helps them to build vocabulary and other necessary skills for successful living.

FIRST NOTES

My Song for Each Day

Jesus wants me for a sunbeam
To shine for Him each day
In every way try to please Him
At home, at school, at play.
A sunbeam (2x)
Jesus wants me for a sunbeam
A sunbeam (2x)
I'll be a sunbeam for Him.

Prayer

I pray, dear God, that You'll send moonbeams
And give me good and pleasant dreams.
Good night, dear God, now I must sleep;
I'll close my eyes and slumber deep.
I know You watch me from above
And cover me with Your sweet love.
Amen.

Lord, give me wisdom that is
profitable to direct and show
me how to beam true
life for You.
Amen.

The First Notes of this book are songs and prayers that you are encouraged to sing and pray each day.

BEDTIME PRAYER

Thank you, Lord, for all the
blessings of the LIGHT.
It is night and time for me to go to sleep.
Let Your angels be by my bedside
To give me good sleep.

He gives His beloved sleep.
Psalm 127:2b

Let them be above me,
To watch over my defenceless head.

*When you lie down, you will not
be afraid; Yes, you will lie down
and your sleep will be sweet.*
Proverbs 3:24

Let them be beneath me,
To prevent me from falling.

*For He shall give His angels charge over you,
To keep you in all your ways.*
Psalm 91:11

And so, when I awake Lord,
My tongue shall sing Thy praise.
Amen.

MORNING THANKS

Lord Jesus, I love You and I thank
You for keeping Your promise.
I am awake to see another dawn.

I lay down and slept; I awoke,
for the Lord sustained me.
Psalm 3:5

Keep me this day, O Lord, I pray, as I
go about my duties at home, at work,
at school, and wherever I go.
For it is only those You have kept
that are free from all dangers.

Trust in the Lord with all your heart, and
lean not on your own understanding;
In all your ways acknowledge Him,
And He shall direct your paths.
Proverbs 3:5–6

A DAILY PRAYER

Through all the dangers of the night,
The Lord doth keep me safe,
To see another morning dawn
And to bow down the knee.

O Lord, I pray: keep me today,
Beneath Thy mighty wings;
Only the ones whom Thou doth keep
Are from all dangers free.

Let all my thoughts and all my deeds
Show I belong to Thee,
So that my light may truly shine
And beam to all the world.

O grant that I ne'er stray from Thee,
Jesus, Saviour Divine,
Until my eyes there shall behold
Thy face for ever more.

"LIVING FOR JESUS is Life's
Greatest Adventure ..."

BEHAVED

The word BEHAVED has been chosen as the theme for this First book of *Living for Jesus series*. Each letter will be used as a lesson in this book. *Behave* means to conduct oneself in a specified way, especially towards others. When we associate ourselves with the things of God and His kingdom, He can help us direct our actions and *behaviour* toward the right path.

The purpose of this book is to show those lifestyles that we can adopt to become closer to God and to *behave* in the manner that He expect us to.

Take a walk with me as you read through these lessons and see the type of *behaviour* that God expects of you.

Memory Verse for The Series of Lessons
*I will **behave** myself wisely in a perfect way.*
(Psalm 101:2a, KJV, emphasis added)

In the space below, write out a prayer that flows from your heart before starting these lessons:

....

....

....

....

....

Story Text: Daniel 3:1–16

The Bible word for the following lessons is **Bold,** which is taken from our theme **B**EHAVED.

BE CONFIDENT

*B*old, is the word taken from our theme, BEHAVED and that's what we will be talking about in this lesson. *Bold* means confident, brave, fearless and courageous. God wants us to be *bold* and courageous. You can *boldly,* confidently, bravely, fearlessly and courageously overcome all obstacles that may come your way today with God on your side.

Those people who do not believe in God are described in the Bible as the wicked because they have nothing to do with God, which is why they live in fear and insecurity. The Bible says in Proverbs 28:1: *"The wicked flee when no man pursueth: but the righteous are bold as a Lion"* (KJV).

Lesson on *Boldness*

There were three Hebrew teenage boys by the names Shadrach, Meshach, and Abednego. During a war, they were among God's people captured in Judah and carried to Babylon by Nebuchadnezzar. Though exiled in a strange land, these boys served God with *boldness.* We will find out more about how these boys *boldly* took a stand for God in our subsequent lessons.

Prayer: Dear Lord, give me the grace to take a stand for you whenever I need to. Amen.

Are you ready for a change of heart if you haven't done so already? Remember the Word of God says that if you are willing, you will eat the good of the land.

In the space below, write out your thoughts on a change of heart:

....

....

....

....

....

....

....

....

....

....

....

....

....

— · — · — · — · — · — · — · — · — · —

Fear not, for I am with you; Be not
dismayed, for I am your God. I will
strengthen you, Yes, I will help you,
I will uphold you with My righteous right hand.
(Isaiah 41:10)

Story Text: Daniel 3:1–16

Lesson on **Boldness** continues ...

YOU HAVE WHAT IT TAKES

Shadrach, Meshach, and Abednego decided to take a *bold* stand by refusing to worship the image Nebuchadnezzar, the king of Babylon, had set up. They knew the consequences of not bowing down to the image, but God had warned against the worship of any image.

What did God say about Himself when He commanded us to worship no other god but Him alone? He said in Exodus 20:5a: *"I the LORD thy God am a jealous God."* He frowns at and punishes all those who worship idols or images. We are to worship only God.

*"And they overcame him by the
blood of the Lamb and by the word of
their testimony, and they did not love their
lives to the death"* (Revelation 12:11).

The above passage is indeed true of these young, brave teenagers! David in the Bible is a good example here. He was *bold* to face Goliath because he trusted in God, who had helped him in the past to kill a lion and a bear.

Prayer: Lord, help me this day to take a stand for You no matter what the consequences may be. Amen!

In what ways can you stand out like Shadrach, Meshach, and Abednego in our world today?

....

....

....

....

....

....

....

....

....

....

....

....

....

....

....

---

*Therefore "Come out from among
them And be separate, says the Lord.
Do not touch what is unclean,
And I will receive you."*
(2 Corinthians 6:17)

Story Text: Daniel 3:17–30

Lesson on *Boldness* continues …

DARE TO TAKE A STAND

Though Shadrach, Meshach, and Abednego were threatened by the king, in *boldness* they stood firm in their decision because they trusted God. In fury, the king decided to throw them into a burning, fiery furnace, which was heated seven times over.

But Jesus had gone into the fire before them and made the fire of no effect on the three teenage boys, who were convinced of the greatness of their God. This miracle surprised King Nebuchadnezzar greatly.

He was left with no choice but to make a firm decree that only the God of Shadrach, Meshach, and Abednego should be served by the entire nation and empire of Babylon from that time onwards. These young boys were promoted by the king to high positions of authority in the province of Babylon because they stood their ground for God.

Take a break at this point and ponder on the lesson.

Prayer: Dear Jesus, please help me to trust You even in the face of adversity. Amen.

Identify a situation in your life where you have to take a stand for Jesus. How can you do this? What might be difficult about taking a stand?

....

....

....

....

....

....

....

....

....

....

....

....

....

....

....

....

*Therefore take up the whole armor of God,
that you may be able to withstand in the
evil day, and having done all, to stand.*
(Ephesians 6:13)

Story Text: Exodus 20:1–6
Lesson on *Boldness* continues …

NO COMPROMISE

*So that we may **boldly** say, The Lord is my helper, and I will not fear what man shall do unto me. (Hebrews 13:6, KJV, emphasis added)*

Shadrach, Meshach, and Abednego no doubt must have made a confession similar to this scripture. Thereafter, these teenage boys were promoted to high positions in Babylon as a result of the decision they made not to worship the image Nebuchadnezzar had set up. Read Daniel 3:24–30.

Truth is, you may not physically bow your head in worship of an image. But anything you love more than God is your idol, like if you love going partying or playing games with friends more than attending services on a Sunday morning, that's the same as worshipping other gods.

Can you imagine yourself being labelled by God as an idol worshipper, all because you did not take a stand?

Key Verse on *Boldness*
Thou shalt have no other gods before me. (Exodus 20:3, KJV)

Like Shadrach, Meshach, and Abednego, you can preach the gospel of Christ by your act of *boldness* and refusal to worship any image or sin against God.

Do you have "idols" in your life? What changes can you make in your life so that God comes first?

....

....

....

....

....

....

....

....

....

....

....

....

....

....

....

— · — · — · — · — · — · — · — · — · —

*But seek first the kingdom of God
and His righteousness, and all these
things shall be added to you.*
(Matthew 6:33)

BRAIN EXERCISES

As we wrap up the lesson on *boldness*, the following are some brain exercises to test your understanding and knowledge of some of the scriptures on *boldness.*

Complete the sentences by filling in the blanks with the correct words from the word bank at the bottom of the page. You can check your answers in the text above.

So that we may___________ say, The________ is my__________, and I will not________ what________ shall____ unto_____ (Hebrews 13:6).

Therefore I make a decree, That________ __________, nation, and________, which speak anything amiss against the______ of___________, __________, and_____________, shall be cut in pieces, and their houses shall be made a dunghill: because there is___________ God that can________ after this sort. Then the king __________ Shadrach, Meshach, and Abednego, in the province of Babylon (Daniel 3:29–30).

Therefore, brethren, having ___________to enter the __________by the blood of Jesus, by a new and living way which He ___________for us, through the veil, that is, His flesh (Hebrews 10:19–20).

Language Shadrach other deliver
promoted do fear helper Boldly Lord man
Abednego me people God Meshach no
every holiest boldness consecrated

NOTES:

....
....
....
....
....
....
....
....
....
....
....
....
....
....
....
....
....
....
....

Let's wrap up the lesson on *boldness* with prayer, Bible study, and worship. As we wrap up, can you recite any of the key verses on *boldness*?

Bible Reference

*And most of the brethren in the Lord, having become confident by my chains, are much more **bold** to speak the word without fear.*
(Philippians 1:14, emphasis added)

Prayer:

L oving Father, I thank You for Your Word that I learnt today. Help me Lord, to serve You with *boldness*, and give me confidence in Your Word. Amen!

Poem on *Boldness*

In boldness I will answer,
I'll stand up for the truth
And don't be fooled,
I once was weak
But now I've got God's strength in me

In your quiet time notebook, if you have one, write down what you have learned in the past lessons on *boldness*. Title your jottings *"Boldness."* Make a pledge on these lessons and write it down as well.

Story Text: 1 Samuel 30:1–6
The Bible word for the following lessons is **Encourage,** which is taken from our theme B*E*HAVED.

ASK GOD, HE KNOWS THE WAY

*E*ncourage yourself in the Lord today as you read through this lesson. To *encourage* is to give courage, support, confidence, or hope to someone. You can *encourage* yourself when you're faced with an unpleasant situation. Somebody who did just that in the Old Testament was David, and we will be learning about him in this lesson and the subsequent lessons.

After David discovered that Saul wanted to kill him, he went into hiding, away from Saul. One day while David was out of town with his men, his enemies took advantage of their absence and took away their wives, children, and property. On their return and seeing what the enemy had done, David and his men became sorrowful and very distressed. Rather than complaining, David inquired of the Lord and *encouraged* himself in the Lord his God. We will learn more about this story in subsequent lessons.

Prayer: Whenever I am faced with difficulties, Lord, help me to remember to go to You in prayer. Amen.

In what ways do you need *encouragement* in your life right now? How can you *encourage* yourself today? How can you *encourage* others?

....
....
....
....
....
....
....
....
....
....
....
....
....
....

Now David was greatly distressed, for the people spoke of stoning him, because the soul of all the people was grieved, every man for his sons and his daughters. But David strengthened himself in the Lord his God.
(1 Samuel 30:6)

Story Text: 1 Samuel 30:1–19

Lesson on **Encouragement** continues ...

DON'T GIVE UP!

The problem David faced was great. But rather than give up and lose hope, he *encouraged* himself and put his faith in God. He asked God what he should do. The Bible put it this way: David inquired of the Lord, saying, "Shall I pursue this troop? Shall I overtake them?" And He answered him, "Pursue, for you shall surely overtake them and without fail recover all." He did what God told him, and eventually "recovered all" that they lost.

You can do the same too. Whenever you are faced with any unpleasant situation in your life, be it with your studies, with friends, or even a breakup of a cherished relationship with a friend, ask God what you should do about the situation.

Nothing is too big or too small to ask God about. Yes, God cares about every detail of your life. If you allow Him, He will help you, just like He helped David.

Key Verse on *Encouragement*

*And he set the priests in their charges and **encouraged** them to the service of the house of the LORD.*
(2 Chronicles 35:2, KJV, emphasis added)

Do you have a problem you need to take to God?
Write a prayer asking Him to help you:

....

....

....

....

....

....

....

....

....

....

....

....

....

....

....

....

....

....

....

---

*Now this is the confidence that we
have in Him, that if we ask anything
according to His will, He hears us.*
(1 John 5:14)

Story Text: Deuteronomy 3:21–29
Lesson on *Encouragement* continues …

MOVE ON IN FAITH

Yesterday, we studied the first lesson on *encouragement*, and we talked about *encouragement* in difficult times.

As much as we need *encouragement* in times of crises, we can also be *encouraged* toward achieving a goal. You may have a project, exam, or task relevant to your career or life's pursuit about which you seem in doubt of your ability to succeed. For instance, you may lack confidence about a project you are about to start, or are nervous whenever a responsibility is given to you, or your fear has something to do with the gigantic size of the task confronting you. All you need is courage!

A Dose of Faith

Your case is similar to what confronted Joshua after Moses, the servant of God, died. Just before Joshua, God had used Moses to accomplish great things both in Egypt and throughout the wilderness journey of the children of Israel. Taking the position of leadership after Moses died, Joshua must have felt small and incapable of the task but God helped him.

Make a list of what you need God's help with:

....

....

....

....

....

....

....

....

....

....

....

....

....

....

....

....

....

....

....

....

*Ask, and it will be given to you; seek, and you
will find; knock, and it will be opened to you.*
(Matthew 7:7)

Story Text: Deuteronomy 3:21–29
Lesson on *Encouragement* continues ...

COURAGE FROM GOD

Taking the position of leadership after Moses died, Joshua must have felt incapable of the task. So, what did God do? God told Moses just before he was taken away to charge Joshua, *encourage* him, and strengthen him. He went further to say that he would go over before the people and cause them to inherit the land that they would see.

Obedience is based on faith. If we truly trust God, we obey Him. Our emotions are not to drive us; instead, we are to obey God, whatever that means. Sometimes the possible consequences of obedience are so enormous that we need great courage to obey God. For many believers throughout the centuries, obedience has meant that they were faced with the possibility of loss or even death. In many cases, they courageously chose to obey God because of their faith, despite the cost. Courage is the decision to choose faith over fear in the face of danger or loss.

Prayer: Lord, give me the grace I need to be courageous and to choose faith over fear, even in the face of danger. Amen.

Reflect on your own past experience. Have you ever let someone talk you into doing the right thing before? What happened afterwards? Were you glad you had listened to their advice?

....
....
....
....
....
....
....
....
....
....
....
....
....
....
....
....
....
....

*Trust in the Lord with all your heart, And
lean not on your own understanding;
In all your ways acknowledge Him,
And He shall direct your paths.*
(Proverbs 3:5–6)

Story Text: Deuteronomy 3:1–21

Lesson on *Encouragement* continues …

CONFIDENCE FROM PAST VICTORIES

You must have heard the saying that experience is the best teacher. Indeed, we learn a lot from our past experiences. If you read Deuteronomy 3:28 in the previous lesson, you realize that it was based on previous successes that Moses could charge Joshua according to God's command to cause the children of Israel to go on to possess the land of promise. I am sure that eventually Joshua was glad he listened to Moses.

Even beyond what Moses said to *encourage* Joshua, God Himself spoke to Joshua: *"Be strong and of good courage, for to this people you shall divide as an inheritance the land which I swore to their fathers to give them"* (Joshua 1:6). As if Joshua did not hear God the first time, God spoke again in verse seven: *"Only be strong and very courageous …"* Then again in verse nine, God repeated for the third time: *"Have I not commanded you? Be strong and of good courage; do not be afraid, nor be dismayed, for the Lord your God is with you wherever you go."*

Prayer: Dear Lord, help me to always remember what You have done for me in the past and believe in You for the future.

How can you *encourage* yourself in the Lord when nothing seems to be going in the right direction?

....

....

....

....

....

....

....

....

....

....

....

....

....

....

Now David was greatly distressed, for the people spoke of stoning him, because the soul of all the people was grieved, every man for his sons and his daughters. But David strengthened himself in the Lord his God.
(1 Samuel 30:6)

Story Text: Deuteronomy 3:1–21

Lesson on *Encouragement* continues …

BE *ENCOURAGED* TODAY!

True *encouragement* can only come from God. Relying upon Jesus Christ in our time of need and listening to that still, small voice of the Holy Spirit is how we can truly receive (and give) *encouragement*.

Encouragement helps to put that fear of the unknown away, and courage is built inside of us to take steps toward achieving that desired goal that otherwise may not be achieved were it not for that act of *encouragement* that came our way. Therefore, be *encouraged* today, overcome your fears, and take steps to achieve that goal you have in mind. Your victory today will make you an *encouragement* to others tomorrow.

Prayer:

Lord, show me how to come out of a problem when all doors seem to be closed, through the power of Your Holy Spirit. Amen.

Key Verse on *Encouragement*

David **encouraged** *himself in the Lord his God.*
(1 Samuel 30:6, KJV, emphasis added)

What goals are you pursuing in your life? How has God's Word *encouraged* you in achieving these goals?

....

....

....

....

....

....

....

....

....

....

....

....

....

....

....

....

....

....

....

....

For God has not given us a spirit of fear, but of power and of love and of a sound mind.
(2 Timothy 1:7)

BRAIN EXERCISES

The following are some brain exercises to test your understanding and knowledge of some of the scriptures on *encouragement.*

Complete the sentences by filling in the blanks with the correct words from the word bank at the bottom of the page. You can check your answers in the lessons.

And he set the priests in their charges and ________________them to the ______________of the ______________of the LORD (2 Chronicles 35:2).

"Have not I commanded thee? Be __________and of a good______________; be not______________, neither be thou______________: for the LORD thy God is with thee withersoever thou__________."

Have I not commanded you? Be ____________ and of good __________; do not be ____________, nor be ________________, for the Lord your God is with you wherever you ____ (Joshua 1:9).

And David was greatly____________; for the people spoke of stoning him because the soul of all the __________was__________, every man for his sons and for his daughters: But David ______________ ____________in the LORD his God (1 Samuel 30:6).

Encouraged strong afraid
dismayed distressed people grieved
courage encouraged himself service go

NOTES

....

....

....

....

....

....

....

....

....

....

....

....

....

....

....

....

....

....

....

....

Let's wrap up the lesson on *encouragement* with prayer, Bible study, and worship. As we wrap up, can you recite any of the key verses on *encouragement?*

Prayer:

Thank You, heavenly Father, for Your Word of *encouragement.* Give me the courage to face situations that may come my way and the power to break through to victory. This I pray, O Lord. Amen.

Bible Reference

*And David was greatly distressed; for the people spake of stoning him because the soul of all the people was grieved, every man for his sons and for his daughters: But David **encouraged** himself in the LORD his God. (1 Samuel 30:6, KJV)*

Poem on *Encouragement*

Encouraged by the Word of God,
Through my sweet Savior's words
The weight is gone; rejoice, it's true!
I'll now encourage all of you.

In your quiet time notebook, if you have one, write down what you have learned in the past lessons on *encouragement.* Title your jottings *"Encourage."* Make a pledge on these lessons and write it down as well.

NOTES

....

....

....

....

....

....

....

....

....

....

....

....

....

....

....

....

....

....

....

....

Story Text: Matthew 22:37-40

The Bible word for the following lessons is **Help,** which is taken from our theme BE_**H**_AVED.

STIR UP ONE ANOTHER IN LOVE

_H_elp, is the word we will be learning about in this lesson. _Help_ means to make it easier for (someone) to do something by offering one's services or resources. The truth is, _help_ and all the words associated with it can only come out of a heart of _love_.

Looking at how God made us all and the things He put on this earth for our use, it should be easy to say He loves us. Can you identify one or two things God has given you to _help_ you live life comfortably? Now try to imagine life without those things! Do you think life would be odd without them? I think so too.

In His life on earth, Jesus showed us the importance of _helping_ others. Think about how you can serve your youth group in church. _Help_ someone who does not know God by introducing them to Him.

Prayer: Dear Lord, I thank you for my life. I know that You have equipped me with knowledge, talent, and resources. I pray that I can use all that You have given to me to _help_ others. Amen.

What is the most *helpful* or kind thing that someone has ever done for you? How did that make you feel?

....

....

....

....

....

....

....

....

....

....

....

....

....

....

....

....

....

....

I have shown you in every way, by laboring like this, that you must support the weak. And remember the words of the Lord Jesus, that He said, 'It is more blessed to give than to receive.
(Acts 20:35)

Story Text: Matthew 22:37-40

Lesson on *Help* continues....

BE WILLING TO GIVE A HELPING HAND

Because by nature we humans tend toward doing bad things more than we want to do good, as a result of the fall of humanity, God gave us a *helpful* resources by giving us a set of rules. One rule is that we should love our neighbour as ourselves. If we love someone, we find ways to *help* that person when necessary. Love is the main driving force that causes us to *help* others in need.

But love that gives us that drive does not just come to our hearts on its own. Hebrews 4:16 *helps* us understand that we need grace and strength from God to *help* others in their time of need.

This scripture says, *"Let us therefore come boldly unto the throne of grace, that we may obtain mercy, and find grace to **help** in time of need"* (Hebrews 4:16, KJV, emphasis added).

Jesus is our perfect example. By washing His disciples' feet, Jesus *helped* his friends in a practical way. We too need to learn to *help* others in practical ways.

Key Verse on *Help*
*But do not forget to do good and to
share, for with such sacrifices God
is well pleased.* (Hebrews 13:16)

Where do you need God's *help* in your life? Write
a prayer asking Him for Grace (*help*):

....

....

....

....

....

....

....

....

....

....

....

....

....

....

....

....

— - — - — - — - — - — - — - — - — - —

*Our soul waits for the Lord; He
is our help and our shield.*
(Psalm 33:20)

Story Text: Luke 10:30–35

Lesson on *Help* continues …

YOU CAN BE THERE FOR A FRIEND

Jesus told a story about a man who *helped* someone in great need. He was known as the Good Samaritan. His story is particularly interesting because the man he *helped* was not a friend, nor did he even know him. To make the matter worse, the man was a Jew, with whom the Samaritans had little in common.

The Jewish man had fallen victim to highway bandits who robbed and beat him up, leaving him half dead by the road. The Bible story states that two highly religious Jews, first a priest and a Levite, saw the wounded man and went their way, failing to *help* their kinsman.

But when the Samaritan man came by, he chose to *help* the wounded man. The Samaritan man acted in love. It didn't matter to him whether or not the wounded man was a Jew or a Samaritan. If that had mattered to him, he probably wouldn't have *helped*. That was indeed an achievement for the Samaritan man. I believe he was glad he had the privilege of *helping* a dying man.

Prayer: Dear God, give me eyes to see those who are in need and give me the ability to *help*. Amen.

What are some obstacles that might be preventing you from *helping?*

....

....

....

....

....

....

....

....

....

....

....

....

————————————————————————————

*What does it profit, my brethren, if someone
says he has faith but does not have works?
Can faith save him? If a brother or sister
is naked and destitute of daily food, and
one of you says to them, "Depart in peace,
be warmed and filled," but you do not give
them the things which are needed for the
body, what does it profit? Thus also faith by
itself, if it does not have works, is dead.*
(James 2:14–17)

**Story Text: Matthew 10:42;
Genesis 24:1–67**

Lesson on *Help* continues …

GIVE AND IT WILL COME BACK TO YOU

Genesis 24 contains a story, similar to the Good Samaritan, about Rebekah, who became the wife of Isaac and mother of Esau and Jacob. She *helped* draw water from the well for Abraham's servant and his camels to drink, with no idea of what his mission was. Little did Rebekah know that her deed of kindness was for her own good. Read Genesis 24:1–67 to get the full story.

Does God reward good deeds done by Christians? The answer is undoubtedly yes—we will definitely be rewarded for doing good, because it is written in Matthew 10:42: *"And whoever gives one of these little ones only a cup of cold water in the name of a disciple, assuredly, I say to you, he shall by no means lose his reward."*

Prayer: Dear Lord, *help* me not to neglect to do good and be kind to those in need of my *help*. Amen.

Who in your life can you *help?* In what ways
would you *help* them?

....

....

....

....

....

....

....

....

....

....

....

....

....

....

....

....

....

— · — · — · — · — · — · — · — · — · —

*Give, and it will be given to you: good
measure, pressed down, shaken together,
and running over will be put into your
bosom. For with the same measure that
you use, it will be measured back to you.*
(Luke 6:38)

Story Text: 2 Chronicles 26:1–15

Lesson on *Help* continues …

GOD GIVES THE GRACE

Going by what we all know of God's *help* for each of us, we should feel guilty if we fail to *help* others; don't you think so? We ought to *help* people in need whenever the opportunity shows up.

But there is absolutely nothing we can do by our own power without God *helping* us. We need God's **help** in all things; even the grace to be willing to do the right thing comes from God, so we need to ask Him for that grace. We are told in 2 Chronicles 26:15 that Uzziah prospered because God marvellously *helped* him. Uzziah was only sixteen years old when he began to reign. Have you ever thought of how a boy of that age was able to rule a whole kingdom? The answer is found in 2 Chronicles 26:4–5. Some highlights from the Bible passage read: "… *he did that which was right in the sight of the LORD … And he sought God … and as long as he sought the LORD, God made him to prosper*" (KJV). This is indeed a mouthful and food for thought.

Prayer: Lord, *help* me to put my trust in You. Amen.

Have you thought of how grateful the needy were that Jesus cared for in the Bible?

What do you remember about the five thousand people Jesus fed?

....

....

....

....

....

....

....

....

....

....

....

....

....

....

....

....

....

....

He who has a generous eye will be blessed,
For he gives of his bread to the poor.
(Proverbs 22:9)

Story Text: 2 Chronicles 26:1–15

Lesson on *Help* continues …

BE A REFLECTION OF GOD'S IMAGE (IN YOU)

Uzziah did not only prosper at home, but out there he won many battles. None of those victories came by his own strength but by the *help* of God. That is the vital lesson we must all learn about achievements and successes. To God be all the glory always!

As for that project you have been struggling with, don't you think all you need is God's *help* and divine direction to make it work out easily?

Knowing that there is no limit to God's *help* for us humans, we should reflect God's image in us to others by exhibiting that same characteristic of God in *helping* others in their time of need, which is what God would do. Make a choice today! Remember, when you make wise choices, you make yourself happy, you make your parents proud of you, and most of all, you make God happy.

Key Verse on *Help*

*God is our refuge and strength, a very present **help** in trouble.* (Psalm 46:1)

Prayer: Lord Jesus, *help* me to prosper in all that I do as I start obeying Your commands by *helping* others in need whenever I am able to do so. Amen.

Don't be reluctant to give a *helping* hand to someone today. What are those challenges that could get in the way of you *helping*?

....

....

....

....

....

....

....

....

....

....

....

....

....

....

....

....

Give to him who asks you, and from him who wants to borrow from you do not turn away.
(Matthew 5:42)

BRAIN EXERCISES

The following are some brain exercises to test your understanding and knowledge of some of the scriptures on *help*.

Complete the sentences by filling in the blanks with the correct words from the word bank at the bottom of the page. You can check your answers in the lessons.

Jesus said unto him, Thou shalt love the Lord thy God with all thy_________, and with all thy______, and with all thy__________. This is the _______and great_________________. And the second is like unto it, Thou shalt love thy_______________ as thyself. On these two commandments hang all the _______and the prophets.

Complete the above from the story text in Matthew 22:37–40.

Let us therefore come _______unto the throne of_______, that we may obtain_______, and find grace to ______in time of_______ (Hebrews 4:16).

God is our _____________and_______________, a very ___________*help* in trouble (Psalm 46:1).

refuge commandment neighbour
mind law need help heart soul first
boldly mercy grace present strength

NOTES

....
....
....
....
....
....
....
....
....
....
....
....
....
....
....
....
....
....
....
....
....

Let's wrap up the lesson on *help* with prayer, Bible study, and worship. As we wrap up, can you recite any of the key verses on *help*?

Prayer:

Dear Lord, it is clear to me that You are my *helper*. *Help* me this day, dear Lord, to show love to others as best as I can in return of Your love for me. Amen.

Bible Reference

Our soul waits for the Lord; He is our help and our shield. (Psalm 33:20)

Poem on *Help*

Sing it over and over again,
Lord, my *helper* in times of need;
Sing it louder and louder again,
I really wish to *help* others in need.

In your quiet time notebook if you have one, write down what you have learned in the past lessons on *help*. Title your jottings "*Help*." Make a pledge on these lessons and write it down as well.

Story Text: Hebrews 10:22–26

The Bible word for the following lessons is **Assembly,** which is taken from our theme BEH_A_VED.

GET INVOLVED

Today's lesson is *Assembly* and it reminds me of fellowship. We should constantly be reminded to not forsake the *assembly* of God's children.

Assembly means gathering or meeting. The Bible tells us in Hebrews 10:25: "*not forsaking the assembling of ourselves together, as is the manner of some, but exhorting one another, and so much the more as you see the Day approaching*". We are encouraged by the Word of God to not neglect the worship of God together with God's people.

Unfortunately, some people do not see the importance of corporate or church worship together, but I tell you, it is a command that God has given to us, His children. If you are already a part of the vibrant youth in God's kingdom, go a step beyond. It is not enough that you attend church services; you must further get involved in the activities in church. This shows commitment on your part. You are not just a member but a committed one.

Prayer: Thank You, Lord, for Your Word and for Your plan of love for mankind. Amen.

David said that he was glad when they said unto him, "Let us go into the house of the Lord." Can you reflect on your church involvement and ways you can become more involved?

....

....

....

....

....

....

....

....

....

....

....

....

....

....

....

....

— · — · — · — · — · — · — · — · —

Oh come, let us worship and bow down;
Let us kneel before the Lord our Maker.
(Psalm 95:6)

Story Text: Hebrews 10:22–26

Lesson on *Assembly* continues ...

BUILD ON THE SOLID ROCK

Do you remember the story of the three little pigs that built their houses on three different platforms? The wisest of them built his of bricks. The others built their houses of hay and sticks. I guess you can tell which house remained standing after the storm came beating on the houses. I tell you, the brick house is like the church. I don't mean the building as much as the people in the building—God's people. The mutual support of loving people in church keeps us safe in the midst of life's troubles. When we come together as children of God and fellowship with one another as one body in Christ, a strong bond is created by the power of the Holy Spirit that cannot be destroyed by the forces of darkness. Praise God!

Prayer: Dear Lord, sometimes I don't feel like waking up for Sunday school. Even though waking up early sometimes isn't convenient, I know it's the right thing to do. So I will do my best to wake up for Sunday school, even when it's hard. Help me, Lord, I pray.

Amen.

Do you know that the saying "United we stand and divided we fall" is actually a true saying? How does this saying apply to your life?

....

....

....

....

....

....

....

....

....

....

....

....

....

....

....

....

....

....

*Let us hold fast the confession of our hope
without wavering, for He who promised is
faithful. And let us consider one another
in order to stir up love and good works,*
(Hebrews 10:23–24)

Story Text: Matthew 16:18-19

Lesson on **Assembly** continues....

IMPORTANCE OF FELLOWSHIP

Going to Church or Sunday school or being a part of a Christian group or fellowship is quite important. Yes, the world and its evil ways, and the devil will come along too, huffing and puffing, but the Church will keep you safe.

Don't skip or miss any Sunday service. To go to any other activity at the time of church service is like building one of those houses of hay and sticks. In the end they will blow away with the wind. Only the Church will stand.

This reminds me of what Jesus says about His Church in Matthew 16:18, *"And I say also unto thee, That thou art Peter, and upon this rock I will build my church; and the gates of hell shall not prevail against it"* (KJV). The Church is unbeatable; and the fire in it is unquenchable.

But what happens to a log if you take it out of a burning fire? That's right – it goes out. If you miss out on the *assembly* of Christians, you too will lose the fire and joy of LIVING FOR JESUS.

Are you ready to be on fire for God? How can you ignite that fire this week?

....

....

....

....

....

....

....

....

....

....

....

....

....

....

....

....

....

....

....

Be strong and of good courage, do not fear nor be afraid of them; for the Lord your God, He is the One who goes with you. He will not leave you nor forsake you."
(Deuteronomy 31:6)

Story Text: Exodus 24:1–3
Lesson on **Assembly** continues …

THE BLESSINGS OF FELLOWSHIP

The lesson on fellowshipping with one another from our previous lesson continues here. The blessings associated with attending church services and fellowships are enormous. It's in church and fellowship, or the *assembly* of God's children, that we exhort one another, and everyone is blessed; it's in *assembly* that we listen to testimonies of God's work of grace in others and faith is stirred up in us to believe that what God has done for one person, He can do for another.

In addition to testimonies, we also share in the messages preached and the worship and prayer sessions by which God reaches out to His children as we *assemble* together. God also sends His Holy Spirit through those messages, touching our lives.

The Israelites usually came together with Moses, their leader, to hear from God on a regular basis. God gave them His laws through this medium. (See Exodus chapters 20, 23, and 24:1–3.) It is a privilege indeed to *assemble* together in worship of this great God.

How do you plan to be more committed to the things of God?

....

....

....

....

....

....

....

....

....

....

....

....

....

....

....

....

....

....

But Daniel purposed in his heart that he would not defile himself with the portion of the king's delicacies, nor with the wine which he drank; therefore he requested of the chief of the eunuchs that he might not defile himself.
(Daniel 1:8)

BRAIN EXERCISES

As we wrap up the lesson on *assembly*, the following are some brain exercises to test your understanding and knowledge of some of the scriptures on *assembly*.

Complete the sentences by filling in the blanks with the correct words from the word bank at the bottom of the page. You can check your answers in the lessons.

Not forsaking the ______________of ourselves together as the ____________of some is; but _____________one another: and so much the more as ye see the day____________" (Hebrews 10:25).

And I say also unto thee, That thou art_________, and upon this_________ I will build my____________; and the ________of hell shall not ____________against it (Matthew 16:18).

And _________came and told the people all the words of the________, and all the_______________: and all the people _____________with one_______, and said, All the words which the Lord hath said will we____________.

Complete the above from the story text in (Exodus 24:3).

> Moses voice church approaching rock
> prevail assembling manner exhorting
> gates do Peter judgments Lord

NOTES

Let's wrap up the lesson on *assembly* with prayer, Bible study, and worship. As we wrap up, can you recite any of the key verses on *assembly*?

Prayer:

Heavenly Father, I thank You for making me who I am. Help me Lord, to be attentive to Your Word and to know what is expected of me. I promise not to engage in unprofitable activities when I ought to be in the *assembly* of God's people. Help me, O Lord, I pray. Amen.

Bible Reference

*"not forsaking the **assembling** of ourselves together, as is the manner of some, but exhorting one another, and so much the more as you see the Day approaching."*
(Hebrews 10:25, emphasis added)

Poem on *Assembly*

Come over, come over,
Assembly Assembly,
Together, together, God commands.

In your quiet time notebook, if you have one, write down what you have learned in the past lessons on *assembly.* Title your jottings *"Assembly."* Make a pledge on these lessons and write it down as well.

NOTES

Story Text: Romans 9:20–24

The Bible word for the following lessons is **Vessel,** which is taken from our theme BEHA<u>V</u>ED.

WHAT *VESSEL* ARE YOU?

V*essel,* is the word for this lesson, taken from our theme word BEHAVED. Today, I surrender myself to the Potter, who makes a *vessel* of honour out of me. I hope you feel the same way.

The word *vessel,* in a special sense, relates to useful household containers like pots, plates, cups, and especially those hand-made by a potter. The lesson therefore relates to a person or thing that conveys or embodies useful qualities beneficial to God and humanity. By the original creation plan, we are all expected to be *vessels* in the hands of our Creator.

God has given you a free will; that is why you are able to make decisions of what you want to do or become in life. But there is a question in the Bible that should puzzle you, found in Romans 9:21: *"Hath not the potter power over the clay, of the same lump to make one **vessel** unto honour and another unto dishonour?"* (KJV, emphasis added). Paul is saying that God has the sovereign power, the unquestionable power, to do unto you what He deems fit, yet He chose to give you the free will to choose what you please. If I may ask, what do you choose? Do you choose to let Him mold you to what He knows you are best in?

Identify the areas in your life that you need to surrender to God:

....

....

....

....

....

....

....

....

....

....

....

....

....

....

....

....

———————————————————————————————

But now, O Lord, You are our Father; We
are the clay, and You our potter; And
all we are the work of Your hand.
(Isaiah 64:8)

Story Text: Romans 9:20–24; Jeremiah 18:4

Lesson on *Vessel* continues …

SEPARATED VESSEL

Many people misuse their free will and choose to do bad things that cause them pain, sorrow, and failure in life. This conduct does not make God happy and He wants to help you. If you yield yourself to God by surrendering your life to Him and letting Him take absolute control over your life, you are giving God a chance to make the best out of your life.

In Jeremiah 18:4, the Bible tells the story of a potter at work: *"And the vessel that he made of clay was marred in the hand of the potter: so he made it again another vessel as seemed good to the potter to make it."* God is the Potter and that *vessel* is you!

Sometimes you are faced with challenges that hinders you from having your way in certain circumstances. It might be God's way of preventing you from getting into trouble. Maybe that thing you're fighting for is not what you need. Only God knows, and if that is the case, it is wiser to let God do what is best for you. In Jeremiah 18:5–6, God told Jeremiah that just like the clay is in the hand of a potter, so are we in His hands. What a beautiful thing to know!

In what ways can you be a *vessel* in the hands
of God?

....

....

....

....

....

....

....

....

....

....

....

....

....

....

....

....

— · — · — · — · — · — · — · — · — · —

But in a great house there are not only
vessels *of gold and silver, but also of*
wood and clay, some for honor and some
for dishonor. Therefore if anyone cleanses
himself from the latter, he will be a **vessel**
for honor, sanctified and useful for the
Master, prepared for every good work.
(2 Timothy 2:20–21)

Story Text: Ephesians 6:1–3

Lesson on *Vessel* continues ...

A *VESSEL* UNTO HONOUR

I f asked by your parents to not do something that you feel is the right thing to do or maybe they encouraged you to do something that perhaps you are hesitant about, just stop and tell yourself, "Maybe God wants it Mummy or Daddy's way." Always see God in those instructions that are given to you. This sort of attitude will guide you from going astray. And remember, there is blessing in obedience!

God intends to make you a *vessel* of honour if you allow Him. Then the world will see you and recognize that there is something unique about you. You will be admired and honoured by people around you because of the way you conduct yourself. The light of God that shines through you as a result of your good conduct will reflect upon others. A good example of someone in the bible that was made a *vessel* of honour is Saul who became Paul from his conversion story. Read Acts 9 to get the full story.

God is absolutely pure and desires that His children be of the same quality too. The Almighty God cannot compromise this standard if He has to find a pure *vessel* to use. Read 1 Peter 1:15–16 and Matthew 5:48. 2 Timothy 2:19 says:

"Nevertheless the foundation of God standeth sure, having this seal; The Lord knoweth them that are his. And, let everyone that nameth the name of Christ depart from iniquity" (KJV).

List ways in which you can be a *vessel* of honour:

....

....

....

....

....

....

....

....

....

....

....

....

....

....

....

....

For we are His workmanship, created in Christ Jesus for good works, which God prepared beforehand that we should walk in them.
(Ephesians 2:10)

Story Text: Romans 9:30–32

Lesson on *Vessel* continues …

GOD CAN MAKE YOU THE BEST "YOU"

Your attitude has a part to play in becoming a *vessel* of honour. The way you react to things that happen to you counts a lot. God knows everything about you, including your attitude. When you try hard to live right and to have a good attitude, God appreciates that. He helps you make the best out of the circumstances of your life as a *vessel* of honour fit for the Master's use.

Read this quotation: *"But we have this treasure in earthen vessels, that the excellence of the power may be of God and not of us. We are hard-pressed on every side, yet not crushed; we are perplexed, but not in despair; persecuted, but not forsaken; struck down, but not destroyed— always carrying about in the body the dying of the Lord Jesus, that the life of Jesus also may be manifested in our body"* (2 Corinthians 4:7–10).

To become a *vessel* of honour does not require works but simply believing on the Lord Jesus Christ and living a righteous lifestyle, as described in Romans 9:30–32. Those who choose to become *vessels* of dishonour are those in society with unruly behaviour who bring shame and disrespect to themselves, their families, and society.

Think of areas in your life where you dishonoured God and how you can change that:

....
....
....
....
....
....
....
....
....
....
....
....
....
....
....
....
....
....
....

Or do you not know that your body is the temple of the Holy Spirit who is in you, whom you have from God, and you are not your own?
(1 Corinthians 6:19)

Story Text: Romans 9:20–22
Lesson on *Vessel* continues …

SPECIAL *VESSEL*

The Lord fashions the *vessel* as He pleases so that He can use it in just the way He intends to. For instance, you don't want a hammer when what you need is a sewing needle. The Lord has very specific things He wants to do with each *vessel*. This is why you should not compare your Christian life with that of Mr. A. God's purpose for your life may not be the same as that of your friend. If you are familiar with the call of Moses, the servant of God, you recall that at the burning bush, Moses decided to surrender himself—not his brother, but himself—as a *vessel* to be used by God. This was not an easy thing for Moses to do, but I believe he knew that God needed him for something special. (See Exodus 3—4). Make a similar decision today and surrender your life for God's use. You can be sure of God's blessings if you do! And remember, God uses all kinds of *vessels*, both the saved and the lost person, the clean and the unclean.

Key Verse on *Vessel*
He is a chosen **vessel** *unto me, to bear
my name before the Gentiles, and kings,
and the children of Israel.* (Acts 9:15)

Make yourself available to the Lord to be a
vessel unto honour qualified for the Master's
use. Make a list of ways you can be that *vessel*:

....

....

....

....

....

....

....

....

....

....

....

....

....

....

....

....

....

....

— · — · — · — · — · — · — · — · — · —

*But the Lord said to him, "Go, for he is a
chosen vessel of Mine to bear My name before
Gentiles, kings, and the children of Israel."*
(Acts 9:15)

BRAIN EXERCISES

As we wrap up the lesson on *vessel,* the following are some brain exercises to test your understanding and knowledge of some of the scriptures on *vessel.*

Complete the sentences by filling in the blanks with the correct words from the word bank at the bottom of the page. You can check your answers in the lessons.

Hath not the __________ power over the clay, of the same lump to make one *vessel* unto __________ and another unto__________? (Romans 9:21).

And the ________ that he made of ______ was marred in the ________ of the potter: so he made it again __________ *vessel* as seemed ________ to the potter to make it (Jeremiah 18:4).

Then the word of the ________ came to me, saying, O house of________, cannot I do with you as this potter? saith the LORD. Behold, as the ________ is in the __________ hand, so are ye in mine________, O house of Israel (Jeremiah 18:5–6).

What shall we say then? That the_______________, which followed not after righteousness, have attained to__________________, even the righteousness which is of________. But Israel, which ________________ after the law of righteousness, hath not attained to the law of__________________. Wherefore? Because they sought it not by faith, but as it were by the works of the law. For they stumbled at that ________________ stone (Romans 9:30–32).

In Romans 9:30–32, Paul explains how the riches of God's glory are shown to people who were once not children of God but are now children of God because they confessed their sins and accepted Christ. Now, they are *vessels* of honour.

gentiles righteousness good vessel
honour Israel hand another potter
hand dishonour LORD clay potter's
righteousness faith stumbling followed

Key Verse on *Vessel*

*Every one of you should know how to possess his **vessel** in sanctification and honour. (1 Thessalonians 4:4, KJV)*

Let's wrap up the lesson on *vessel* with prayer, Bible study, and worship. As we wrap up, can you recite any of the key verses on *vessel*?

Prayer:

Loving Saviour, I know that Your thoughts toward me are thoughts of good and not of evil, to bring me to an expected end. So, dear Lord, I want You to make of me a **vessel** of honour and not of dishonour in order for me to have an expected end. Amen.

Bible Reference

*And the **vessel** that he made of clay was marred in the hand of the potter: so he made it again another **vessel** as seemed good to the potter to make it.* (Jeremiah 18:4)

Worship Song on *Vessel*

(*Make a tune for this song*)
Hallelujah, yes, 'tis me,
A **vessel** of honour made of me,
A **vessel** of honour, yes 'tis me.
Hallelujah, yes, 'tis me.

In your quiet time notebook, if you have one, write down what you have learned in the past lessons on *vessel*. Title your jottings *"Vessel."* Make a pledge on these lessons and write it down as well.

NOTES

Story Text: 2 Corinthians 13:5–8

The Bible word for the following lessons is **Examine,** which is taken from our theme BEHAV**E**D.

ARE YOU BORN AGAIN?

Examine, is the word for this lesson, coined from our theme word BEHAVED. *Examine* means to investigate, look at closely, ask questions.

When we are out of line with Christian standards, we ought to ask ourselves, "Am I a true Christian or a counterfeit? Have I given my life to Christ, or am I only putting up a front?" As Christians, we should *examine* ourselves occasionally, especially if there is any kind of wrong behaviour involved.

The fact that the apostle could ask a question like that indicates that there is something that marks true Christianity. A Christian, of course, is not simply one who joins a Christian church, nor does consistently reading the Bible make you a Christian. A true Christian is someone in whom Christ dwells. Paul is suggesting that we ask ourselves if we have the evidence that Jesus Christ lives in us.

What do you do if guilt wells up in your heart because of certain misbehaviour? You ought to pray. Simply say, "I'm sorry, Lord!" and be sure to receive forgiveness when the Holy Spirit bears witness with your spirit that you're forgiven.

Learn to ask God for pardon when you realize you've done something wrong.

What evidence do you have that Jesus Christ lives in you?

....

....

....

....

....

....

....

....

....

....

....

....

....

....

....

....

....

For as many as are led by the Spirit
of God, these are sons of God.
(Romans 8:14)

**Story Text: Psalms 26:1–5;
1 Timothy 5:24–25**

Lesson on **Examine** continues ...

GOD SEES THE HEART

We all know what it feels like to be seen by others when we are doing odd things, like calling people names and being mean to others. No one likes that. But it does us great good to know we are being watched by a prying eye. That keeps us from doing bad things, doesn't it?

Some don't know, but it is to keep us from doing evil that God gave all of us conscience. You know conscience, don't you? It is that present awareness in your heart that tells you whether you have done something right or wrong.

What do you do the moment your conscience rings out the alarm bell in your heart? The moment you notice that you are erring, or you have done something wrong, open up to God in confession and ask Him for forgiveness. Don't cover up your wrongdoings!

Key Verse on *Examine*
*But let a man **examine** himself ...*
(1 Corinthians 11:28a).

Take a few moments to *examine* your conscience.

List the things that you need to make amends on:

....

....

....

....

....

....

....

....

....

....

....

....

....

....

....

....

....

....

....

— - — - — - — - — - — - — - — - — - —

*If we confess our sins, He is faithful
and just to forgive us our sins and to
cleanse us from all unrighteousness.*
(1 John 1:9)

**Story Text: Psalms 26:1–5;
1 Timothy 5:24–25**
Lesson on *Examine* continues ...

EXAMINE ME, O LORD

Have you ever thought of what God sees when He looks at your heart? Does He see a repentant heart? A heart that is willing to say sorry to others when at fault? Jonah had to *examine* himself while he was in the fish's belly. Don't wait to be in a similar situation as Jonah before you begin to seek the face of God. Make it a lifestyle to always inspect your spiritual standing with God.

Key Verse on *Examine*

*Some men's sins are open beforehand,
going before to judgment; and some men
they follow after.* (1 Timothy 5:24, KJV)

One prayer we should learn to pray each day is the prayer of the psalmist: **"*Examine* me, O LORD, and prove me; try my reins and my heart"** (Psalm 26:2, KJV, emphasis added). God expects us to confess our sins to Him; when you confess your sins, you open them up before the judgement seat of Christ, and they are forgiven because you truly confessed and repented of them.

How can you make a habit of self-*examination?*

....

....

....

....

....

....

....

....

....

....

....

....

....

....

....

....

....

He who says, "I know Him," and does not keep His commandments, is a liar, and the truth is not in him. But whoever keeps His word, truly the love of God is perfected in him. By this we know that we are in Him. He who says he abides in Him ought himself also to walk just as He walked.
(1 John 2:4–6)

Story Text: 1 John 1:6–10

Lesson on **Examine** continues …

WHAT IS YOUR STATUS?

1 John 1:9 is a very helpful scripture that tells us what to do after we have *examined* our hearts and feel convicted of sin. It says: *"If we confess our sins, he is faithful and just to forgive us our sins, and to cleanse us from all unrighteousness."* This is about getting a wash from God.

It is similar to what we do when a valuable item gets lost in the mud; when it's found, it's given a good wash. This is the same way God cleanses us up when we come to Him. He cleanses us from all unrighteousness, and we are spiritually clean and happy again.

Perhaps you used bad language at someone, or you hurt someone's feelings. There is still room to confess your faults one to another (James 5:16). Unfortunately, some people don't care about the way they live their lives as Christians; they dwell in their sins. These are people whose sins will follow them to judgement, as we are warned in 1 Timothy 5:24.

Instead of their sins going before them to judgement through confession, the evil that they commit follows them to be judged and condemned. Don't let this happen to you.

Is there someone you need to make amends with? Make a list of how you can work through forgiving others:

....

....

....

....

....

....

....

....

....

....

....

....

....

....

....

Bearing with one another, and forgiving one another, if anyone has a complaint against another; even as Christ forgave you, so you also must do.
(Colossians 3:13)

Story Text: 1 John 1:6–10

Lesson on *Examine* continues ...

DO YOU HAVE A RIGHT ATTITUDE?

Our happiness in life depends a great deal on our attitudes. Our attitude toward ourselves is perhaps the most important attitude of all because it has such a profound effect on our lives. For this reason, we should be careful of our actions and always ask the Lord for His help through His Holy Spirit's guidance.

Jonah's negative attitude and response to God's call landed him in the whale's belly, but thanks be to God for God's mercy that made the opportunity available to him, even in the fish's belly, to *examine* himself and ask for forgiveness and a second chance. (Jonah 2:1–2). God's mercy was extended to Jonah in the fish's belly even though he acted late. It's not yet late for you if you repent and confess your sins to God today. Right now, in God's mercy, He will forgive and cleanse you by the blood of Jesus Christ.

All you need do now is *examine* yourself in the particular situation you are in right now and let God have His way in your life!

*If we confess our sins, He is faithful
and just to forgive us our sins and to
cleanse us from all unrighteousness
(1 John 1:9).*

List areas in which you are not living in God's
will and how you can move into His will more:

....

....

....

....

....

....

....

....

....

....

....

....

....

....

....

....

---

*Not everyone who says to Me, "Lord, Lord,"
shall enter the kingdom of heaven, but he
who does the will of My Father in heaven.*
(Matthew 7:21)

BRAIN EXERCISES

Today as we wrap up the lesson on *examine,* the following are some brain exercises to test your understanding and knowledge of some of the scriptures on *examine.*

Complete the sentences by filling in the blanks with the correct words from the word bank at the bottom of the page. You can check your answers in the lessons.

______________ yourselves as to whether you are in the faith. _______ yourselves. Do you not know yourselves, that _______ _______ is in you?—unless indeed you are ______________ (2 Corinthians 13:5).

Wherefore whosoever shall eat this _______, and drink this cup of the _______, ______________, shall be _______of the body and blood of the Lord. But let a man ______________ himself, and so let him eat of that bread, and _______ of that cup (1 Corinthians 11:27–28).

Vindicate me, O Lord, For I have _______in my integrity. I have also _______in the Lord; I shall not slip. *Examine* me, O Lord, and prove me; Try my mind and my heart. For Your ______________is before my eyes, And I have walked in Your_______ (Psalm 26:1–3).

Jesus Christ Examine Lord disqualified drink unworthily Test bread examine guilty walked trusted lovingkindness truth

NOTES

Let's wrap up the lesson on *examine* with prayer, Bible study, and worship. As we wrap up, can you recite any of the key verses on *examine*?

Prayer:

Lord, I want to fellowship with You. I know that I cannot eat of that bread and drink of that cup if I am found unworthy. So, dear Lord, help me to *examine* myself and be in right standing with You. This I pray, O Lord. Amen.

Bible Reference

Examine yourselves as to whether you are in the faith. Test yourselves. Do you not know yourselves, that Jesus Christ is in you? —unless indeed you are disqualified.
(2 Corinthians 13:5, emphasis added)

Worship Song on *Examine*

(Make a tune for this song)
Examine me, dear Lord, I pray,
Is there a wicked way in me?
Your love to me day after day,
I need You to *examine* me.

In your quiet time notebook, if you have one, write down what you have learned in the past lessons on *examine*. Title your jottings "*Examine*." Make a pledge on these lessons and write it down as well.

NOTES

Story Text: Genesis 1:26–28

The Bible word for the following lessons is **Dominion,** which is taken from our theme BEHAVE**D**.

YOU'RE IN CHARGE!

We have now come to the last letter in our theme word BEHAVED.' I take *dominion* this day over all circumstances through the help of God. The word *dominion* reminds me of Genesis 1:26: *"Then God said, 'Let Us make man in Our image, according to Our likeness; let them have* **dominion** *over the fish of the sea, over the birds of the air, and over the cattle, over all the earth and over every creeping thing that creeps on the earth"* (emphasis added).

Dominion means to rule. Have you ever been told these words: "You're in charge"? How did you feel when you heard those words? I bet you felt good and like someone important. When you're put in charge of something, you are like a king or queen reigning over that thing. From the beginning, God desired that we have *dominion* over everything around us, including all circumstances, whatever they are.

Do you know that you are made in God's image? Have you ever thought of what that means? It means you are like God and can make things happen just like He does, but only if you believe you can. He even put you in charge of all that He has created. Aren't you special? Sure, you are!

What are some challenges in your life that you need to overcome?

....

....

....

....

....

....

....

....

....

....

....

....

....

....

....

Ye are of God, little children, and have
overcome them: because greater is he that
is in you, than he that is in the world.
(1 John 4:4, KJV)

Story Text: Psalms 8:4–9

Lesson on *Dominion* continues …

WHAT DO YOU SEE IN YOURSELF?

Ever read Psalm 8 before? Verses 4–9 tell us that God actually wanted us to be in charge of all the things He created. We ought to be rulers and controllers of situations around us and not the other way around.

Jesus was able to walk upon the sea, teaching us by example to take *dominion* through faith in God. That account is found in John 6:16–21. The sea can be likened to difficult situations around you, such as reading to pass your exams, not having enough to take care of your immediate needs, the fear of rejection, anxiety, and many other concerns. You should be able to walk through them by the help of God only if you believe in His Word. Think of ways that you can affect other people's lives positively by your special you!

Key Verse on *Dominion*

*Order my steps in thy word: and let not any iniquity have **dominion** over me.*
(Psalm 119:133, KJV, emphasis added)

What are those sins you need to take *dominion* over?

———————————————————————————

*Be strong and of good courage, do not fear
nor be afraid of them; for the Lord your
God, He is the One who goes with you.
He will not leave you nor forsake you.*
(Deuteronomy 31:6)

Story Text: Psalms 8:4–9

Lesson on *Dominion* continues …

YOU ARE WHAT YOU BELIEVE YOU ARE

If you think you cannot do something, then you probably will not do it. But if you think you can do something, you are more likely to get it done. It is based on how you feel about yourself that circumstances will respond to you. What we think determines what we do and what we feel. We are controlled by the way we inwardly see and believe things to be. This is what the Bible means when it says, *"As he thinks in his heart, so is he"* (Proverbs 23:7).

To be in charge, you shouldn't quit at the first sign of defeat. If you are having trouble getting something done, don't get frustrated. Don't be discouraged, and don't give up. Just keep trying and believing in yourself. You can really do amazing things when you try hard and keep trying. Remember, don't quit at the first sign of trouble.

Key Verse on *Dominion*:

*You have made him to have **dominion** over the works of Your hands; You have put all things under his feet.* (Psalm 8:6, emphasis added)

Are you trusting God in that situation? Tell Him about it:

....

....

....

....

....

....

....

....

....

....

....

....

....

....

....

....

....

....

You will not need to fight in this battle. Position yourselves, stand still and see the salvation of the Lord, who is with you, O Judah and Jerusalem!' Do not fear or be dismayed; tomorrow go out against them, for the Lord is with you.
(2 Chronicles 20:17)

Story Text: 2 Corinthians 5:17–21; Genesis 1:26-28

Lesson on ***Dominion*** continues ...

YOU HAVE WHAT IT TAKES

I presume that you are born again already and can confidently say you are a child of God. I hope you are, because I don't see how any right-thinking person would want to live without Christ in their lives. People who are drawn to Christ by the Holy Spirit are born again. They live in *dominion* by the help of Christ in them.

In Christ, you have *dominion* and should not give room to friends to intimidate you, run you down, or make you feel bad for not doing the things they do or for any such reasons.

Be in charge, even in situations that are uncomfortable. You may be experiencing bad times at the moment, or you may have experienced bad times in the past, but you must take charge of those circumstances. Don't allow the feeling of guilt to overtake you if you have not sinned against God. Was there a time in your life when you were fearful of the future and you reacted in response to that fear? The devil may want to make you believe that you are responsible for sins you have not committed, or for the unpleasant events around you. Remember, he is a liar and the father of all liars.

Why do you think it's hard to let go of control and trust God for your future?

....

....

....

....

....

....

....

....

....

....

....

....

....

....

....

....

....

....

....

....

Casting all your care upon Him,
for He cares for you.
(1 Peter 5:7)

Story Text: 2 Corinthians 5:17–21; Psalm 8:6

Lesson on *Dominion* continues ...

YOU'VE GOT THIS!

Don't believe in the devil's whispers. All he wants is to get you discouraged and distracted from your focus. As long as you have accepted Christ as your Lord and Saviour, there is nothing to worry about. God has already put inside of you what it takes to overcome all things, even peer/social pressures or whatever it may be.

To everyone who is a new creature in Christ, the Bible says that *"old things are passed away; behold, all things are become new"* (2 Corinthians 5:17b). The past is already gone; don't let the events of the past control your life. Take charge of the day that is before you. Be bold to say no to thoughts and suggestions that do not glorify God. Take control and a firm stand on your decisions and convictions according to how the Holy Spirit leads you.

Key Verse on *Dominion*

*You have made him to have **dominion** over the works of Your hands; You have put all things under his feet.* (Psalm 8:6, emphasis added)

How can you begin to exercise the authority
that God has given to you and be in charge?

....

....

....

....

....

....

....

....

....

....

....

....

....

....

....

....

....

....

*Behold, I give you the authority to
trample on serpents and scorpions, and
over all the power of the enemy, and
nothing shall by any means hurt you.*
(Luke 10:19)

BRAIN EXERCISES

Today, as we wrap up the lesson on *dominion*, the following are some brain exercises to test your understanding and knowledge of some of the scriptures on *dominion.*

Complete the sentences by filling in the blanks with the correct words from the word bank at the bottom of the page. You can check your answers in the lessons.

Then God said, "Let Us make man in Our __________, according to Our _____________; let them have _____________ over the _______ of the sea, over the birds of the _____, and over the cattle, over all the _______ and over every _____________ _______ that creeps on the earth" (Genesis 1:26).

Order my _______ in thy_________: and let not any________ have *dominion* over me (Psalms 119:133).

You have made him to have *dominion* over the _________ of Your hands; You have put all things under his________ (Psalm 8:6).

Then God blessed them, and God said to them, "Be _________ and ________; fill the earth and _________ it; have *dominion* over the fish of the sea, over the birds of the air, and over _______ _______ _______ that moves on the earth" (Genesis 1:28).

Image feet fish earth iniquity dominion air word likeness creeping thing multiply steps works every living thing fruitful subdue

NOTES

....

....

....

....

....

....

....

....

....

....

....

....

....

....

....

....

....

....

....

....

Let's wrap up the lesson on *dominion* with prayer, Bible study, and worship. As we wrap up, can you recite any of the key verses on *dominion*?

Prayer:

Thank You, Father, for the opportunity I have to speak to You today. Thank You for giving me *dominion* over every situation. Amen.

Bible Reference

Then God blessed them, and God said to them, "Be fruitful and multiply; fill the earth and subdue it; have **dominion** *over the fish of the sea, over the birds of the air, and over every living thing that [a] moves on the earth."* (Genesis 1:28)

Poem on *Dominion*

Dominion over all I care,
This Lord, Your Will for me I know,
The trumpet shall not call "Retreat,"
I shall **dominate** and reign.

In your quiet time notebook, if you have one, write down what you have learned in the past lessons on *dominion*. Title your jottings *"Dominion."* Make a pledge on these lessons and write it down as well.

Search for the following words and their beginning letters in the Word Puzzle below:

Bold

Encourage

Help

Assembly

Vessel

Examine

Dominion

WORD PUZZLE

V	A	R	W	A	Q	L	M	U	P	Q	J
A	D	O	E	O	C	L	P	L	L	V	B
W	U	S	W	C	N	U	V	J	Y	D	P
H	N	B	O	L	D	D	N	C	E	Z	O
J	W	E	N	C	O	U	R	A	G	E	I
D	M	H	E	L	P	J	Y	G	S	J	D
A	L	A	S	S	E	M	B	L	Y	O	A
W	J	V	E	S	S	E	L	X	U	Q	V
N	X	E	X	A	M	I	N	E	U	N	U
B	Q	D	O	M	I	N	I	O	N	H	K
Z	J	O	Q	K	D	J	B	P	V	P	K
M	W	D	C	N	W	G	A	T	A	N	L

Answer to word puzzle is found in
the last page of this book.

Behaved

From the statements below, set up a quiz between you and your friends and family members who have read this same book with you. Get your answers cross-checked from the lessons and score yourselves. Have fun!

BOLDNESS

- The names of the three teenagers who refused to bow down to king Nebuchadnezzar's image.
- The stand these young boys took for God.
- Something happened before these boys were thrown into the burning, fiery furnace.
- The king's reaction as a result of God's intervention.
- The lesson talked about things that people love more than God.
- David was bold to face Goliath because he trusted in God, who had helped him in the past.
- The following was said in Exodus 20:5, *"I the LORD thy God am a jealous God."*
- The three Hebrew boys were promoted by the king to high positions of authority in the province of Babylon.

bEhaved

From the statements below, set up a quiz between you and your friends and family members who have read this same book with you. Get your answers cross-checked from the lessons and score yourselves. Have fun!

ENCOURAGE

- Reacting to unfavourable situations, as explained in this lesson.
- Steps to take in trying situations.
- When David's enemies took away his men's wives, children, and property.
- When faced with unpleasant situations in life.
- Joshua taking the position of leadership after Moses died.
- What this lesson says about our confidence.
- What this lesson says about our emotions.
- What God told Moses to do to Joshua just before Moses was taken away.
- When you lack confidence about a project you are about to start, or are nervous whenever a responsibility is given to you.

beHaved

From the statements below, set up a quiz between you and your friends or family members who have read this same book with you. Get your answers cross-checked from the lessons and score yourselves. Have fun!

HELP

- God gave us a set of rules.
- *Helping* in your community.
- Jesus our perfect example.
- The Good Samaritan man was remarkable.
- Rebekah's kindness was for her own good.
- Cup of cold water.
- By nature, we humans tend toward doing bad things more than we want to do good.
- Love is the main driving force that causes us to *help* others in need.
- By washing His disciples' feet, Jesus *helped* his friends in a practical way.
- The Samaritan man acted in love.
- To make the matter worse, the wounded man was a Jew, with whom the Samaritans had little in common.

behAved

From the statements below, set up a quiz between you and your friends or family members who have read this same book with you. Get your answers cross-checked from the lessons and score yourselves. Have fun!

ASSEMBLY

- The story of the three people who built their houses on different platforms.
- Attending church services.
- When you take a log out of a burning fire.
- The following was said in Matthew 16:18, KJV: *"And I say also unto thee, That thou art Peter, and upon this rock I will build my church; and the gates of hell shall not prevail against it."*
- How the Israelites come together in worship and how they hear from God under the leadership of Moses.
- David said that he was glad when they said unto him, "Let us go into the house of the Lord."
- It is not enough that you attend church services.
- The brick house is like the church.

behaVed

From the statements below, set up a quiz between you and your friends or family members who have read this same book with you. Get your answers cross-checked from the lessons and score yourselves. Have fun!

VESSEL

- God has absolute power over us, but He decided to leave us with our own will.
- God's intention for us.
- The *vessel* of honour and the *vessel* of dishonour.
- When you are faced with some challenges that are preventing you from having your way in certain circumstances.
- By the original creation plan, we are all *vessels* in the hands of our Creator.
- Steps to becoming a *vessel* of honour.
- The part your attitude plays when talking about a *vessel* of honour.
- When you yield yourself to God by surrendering your life to Him and letting Him take absolute control over your life.
- When you try hard to live right and to have a good attitude.

behavEd

From the statements below, set up a quiz between you and your friends or family members who have read this same book with you. Get your answers cross-checked from the lessons and score yourselves. Have fun!

EXAMINE

- Evaluating yourself to know if you are living righteously on a daily basis.
- The voice that you have inside of you that puts you in check.
- Here is what 1 Timothy 5:24 says: "*Some men's sins are open beforehand, going before to judgment; and some men they follow after.*"
- When condemnation wells up in your heart because of certain misbehaviour.
- The awareness in your heart that tells you whether you have done something right or wrong.
- What 1 John 2:4–6 says about whoever keeps God's Word.
- Jonah's negative attitude and response to God's call landed him in the whale's belly.

behaveD

From the statements below, set up a quiz between you and your friends or family members who have read this same book with you. Get your answers cross-checked from the lessons and score yourselves. Have fun!

DOMINION

- Genesis 1:26 shows that God wanted you to be in charge of everything around you.
- What the sea that Jesus walked upon is likened to.
- How you are expected to emulate Jesus' example.
- What God desired for us from the beginning of creation according to this lesson.
- When you're told that you are made in God's image.
- What the Bible means when it says, *"For as he thinks in his heart, so is he"* (Proverbs 23:7)
- What the lesson says about not allowing the feeling of guilt overtake you if you know that you have not sinned against God.
- When you're put in charge of something, you are like a king or queen reigning over that thing.

LAST NOTES

Sometimes it appears hard to live as a Christian. Your friends will not always understand why you make choices different from theirs or live in a God-fearing manner. But never give up.

Keep on LIVING FOR JESUS.

Show by your life and words that you belong to the Lord Jesus.

Being a Christian is LIVING OUT what one believes inside.

Remember, "LIVING FOR JESUS is Life's Greatest Adventure."

BEDTIME PRAYER

LORD, keep me while I sleep
From dangers all around.
When I am asleep,
My heart is awake to watch
And pray to Thee.

I will both lie down in peace, and sleep;
For You alone, O Lord, make me
dwell in safety. Psalm 4:8

A prayer presumed to be one's heart desire
even while asleep.

The All-Sufficient in time of need.
The whispering voice that shows the way.
The Unseen Friend at every meal.
The Silent Listener to every Conversation.
The Peace-Loving God that
drives away all fears.

ANSWER TO WORD PUZZLE IN HIGHLIGHTS

V	A	R	W	A	Q	L	M	U	P	Q	J
A	D	O	E	O	C	L	P	L	L	V	B
W	U	S	W	C	N	U	V	J	Y	D	P
H	N	**B**	**O**	**L**	**D**	D	N	C	E	Z	O
J	W	**E**	**N**	**C**	**O**	**U**	**R**	**A**	**G**	**E**	I
D	M	**H**	**E**	**L**	**P**	J	Y	G	S	J	D
A	L	**A**	**S**	**S**	**E**	**M**	**B**	**L**	**Y**	O	A
W	J	**V**	**E**	**S**	**S**	**E**	**L**	X	U	Q	V
N	X	**E**	**X**	**A**	**M**	**I**	**N**	**E**	U	N	U
B	Q	**D**	**O**	**M**	**I**	**N**	**I**	**O**	**N**	H	K
Z	J	O	Q	K	D	J	B	P	V	P	K
M	W	D	C	N	W	G	A	T	A	N	L

BOLD

ENCOURAGE

HELP

ASSEMBLY

VESSEL

EXAMINE

DOMINION